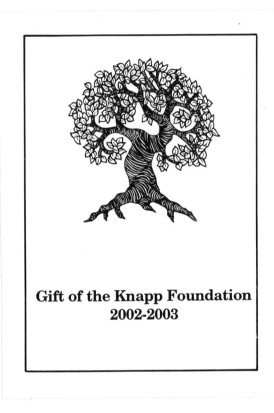

Sanctuaries

Sanctuaries

Peter C. Stone

THE WRITERS' COLLECTIVE

Sanctuaries   by Peter C. Stone

Design and layout   MyLinda Butterworth
Photography   Clive Russ
Photography and digital imaging   Christopher Benson

13 12 11 10 09 08 07 06 05 04 03   5 4 3 2 1

Library of Congress Cataloging-in-Publication Data

Stone, Peter C., 1955-
 Sanctuaries / Peter C. Stone.
    p. cm.
  ISBN 1-932133-50-X (TP : alk. paper)
 1. Stone, Peter C., 1955- 2. New England—In art. I. Title.
  ND237.S7934A4 2003
  759.13—dc21
                        2003000609

Published by The Writers' Collective • Cranston, R.I.

for Sara and Oliver

Acknowledgements

Many people have encouraged me to continue with my work on this story over the past decade. I am grateful to them all. Especially, my family, Amanda, Sara, and Oliver.

Thanks as well to Clive Russ and Christopher Benson for their photography of the paintings, and Meredith Phelan for her early input and representation. Thanks also to Temple Hill Press for their support, and to Lisa Grant and TWC for shepherding this project.

Ramona Peters kindly shared her words from the homepage for The Wampanoag, People of the First Light, at the website of The Children's Museum, Boston.

I am genuinely indebted to Marcella Hague for her enthusiasm and criticism while representing the story in its more recent form, and to Linda Coombs, for her generosity and heartfelt interest.

This is offered with much appreciation for the vast efforts of those involved with land trusts and conservation coalitions, not just in the Wampanoag Homeland, but far beyond. Mostly, it is for the People of the Wampanoag Nation, past and present, and their sacred relationship with the lands and waters that uphold us.

Foreword

The People of the Wampanoag Nation live in the territory of what is now called Cape Cod and the islands of Nantucket and Martha's Vineyard, west to Narragansett Bay and the Providence River. Their lands extend north toward the Great Blue Hills and the southern boundary of the Massachusett Nation.

They are allied in spiritual kinship with the wolf.

The Pilgrims and others settled within this region, the Wampanoag Homeland.

Any sort of landscape is a condition of the soul.
— H. F. Amiel

We name ourselves after the land we live with. Because, not only are we breathing in, we are also drinking from the water that is flavored by that very land. Whatever is deposited in the soil is in that water is in us. So we are all one thing, and we name ourselves after the place that is our nurturing. That sustains our life.

— Ramona Peters, Mashpee Wampanoag

... I am the taste of pure water and the radiance of the sun and moon. I am the sacred word and the sound heard in air, and the courage of human beings.

— The Bhagavad Ghita; Ch. VII: V. 8

Colours are the deeds and sufferings of Light.

— Johann Wolfgang von Goethe

This they tell, and whether it happened so or not I do not know; but if you think about it, you can see that it is true.

— Nick Black Elk

My grandfathers
lived here.

As they do now,

in a wondrous way.

These fields grow splendid circles of hay, from soil that my grandmothers fertilized with dead herring and planted when the oak leaves are the size of a mouse's ear.

In this place the tenderness of moonlight deserves to be loved, haunting as it soothes the hollows of our hearts. Where the meaning of this land is as it ever was,

17

And a sigh stirs forth
when the sun rises
from the water.

This is the home of my grandfathers, the *Wampanoag*, the Eastern People. The People of the First Light.

Here the flowers are our sisters and the rivers move with the blood of my people.

In the shrinking days of falling leaves, I walk the riverbanks that remain. I smell humus and pine and burnished land. I hear the cry of the Red-tailed Hawk.

I tremble in delightful awe.

In the winter my steps crunch softly in the snow beside the memory of footprints of the wolf.

The bare trees clatter and sway.

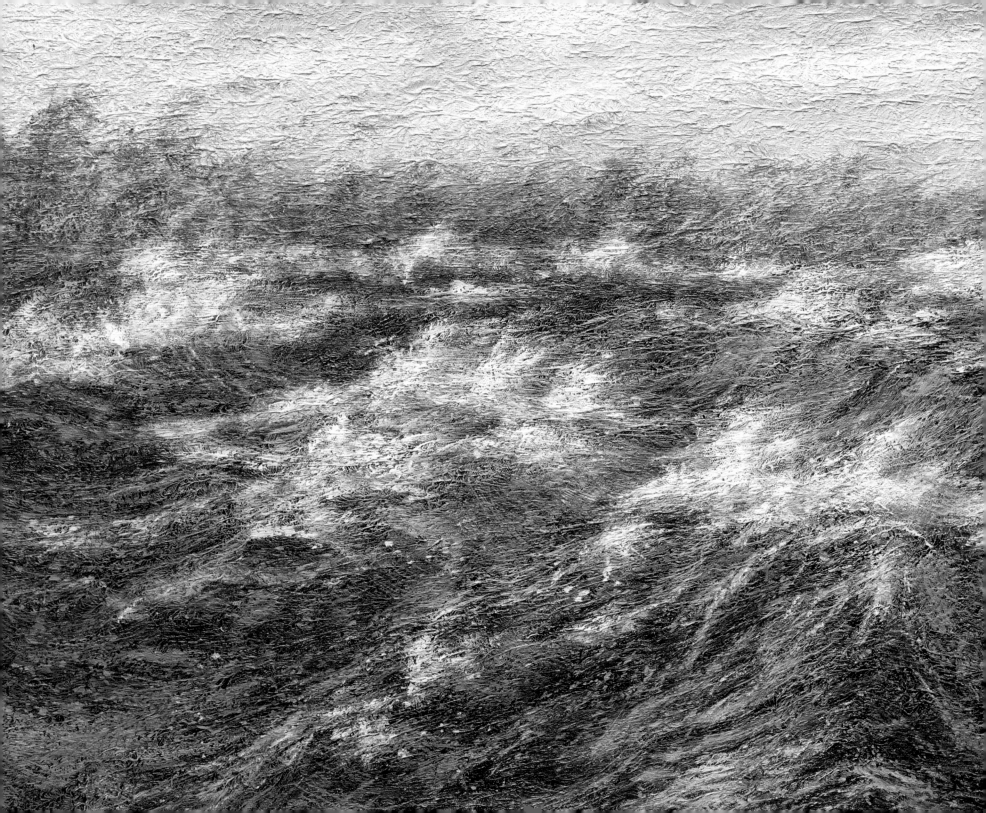

But, no matter how raw the spring floods or howling nor'easters,

Those of us who live here know that when the air turns powdered with haze

The humid days will grow long and mild.

And balmy sou'westers will blow carefree across the saltmeadows again.

My grandfathers and I are custodians of this precious land. We listen to the heartbeat of the seasons and care for the earth that bears life.

For the children of our children. For their innocent laughter.

For when we walk along the shore, or through the woods and fields, the sun drips from each leaf and shimmers on the grasses.

Osprey cries, Fish rises, and Deer hesitates in the underbrush.

I see and hear these echoes.
And rejoice for the sanctuaries of
my grandfathers that still exist.

Come, celebrate them in the hidden vistas
beyond the edge of a winding dirt road,

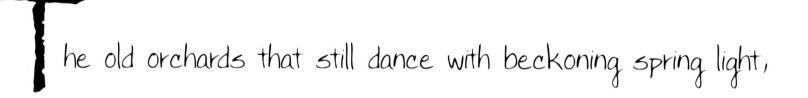The old orchards that still dance with beckoning spring light,

The swamplands and bogs bright with wild cranberries.

Walk these woods still standing

And meadows unspoiled.

For it is true.
Just as no sacred name has
ever lost its meaning.

Our people lived here.
As they do now, in a wondrous way.

Index of Paintings with the Artist's Notes
Oils on Canvas

Selected Bibliography

Bradford, William: *Of Plymouth Plantation 1620-1647*, edited by Samuel Eliot Morrison, Alfred A. Knopf, 1952.

Cook, Sherburne: *The Indian Population of New England in the Seventeenth Century*, Berkeley, 1976.

Church, Benjamin: *The History of King Philip's War*, Dexter, 1865.

Eliot, John: *Indian Dialogues*, edited by Henry W. Bowden and James P. Ronda; Greenwich Press, London, 1980.

Jacobs, Wilbur R.: *Dispossessing the American Indian: Indians and Whites on the Colonial Frontier*, New York, 1972.

The Old Dartmouth Historical Sketches, Volume III; 1903.

Travers, Milton A.: *The Wampanoag Indian Federation*, The Christopher Publishing House, Boston, 1957. (revised edition copyright 1961)

Ordering *Sanctuaries*

For more information about limited edition prints from the book, or to order direct,

visit http://www.PeterCStoneStudios.com

To contact the author, email: pstone@writerscollective.org

For information about the Wampanoag Homeland and People of the First Light,

visit: http://www.bostonkids.org and www.plimoth.org.